Day at the Zoo

Nonstandard Measurement

Joshua Rae Martin

Publishing Credits

Dona Herweck Rice, *Editor-in-Chief*; Lee Aucoin, *Creative Director*; Don Tran, *Print Production Manager*; Sara Johnson, *Senior Editor*; Jamey Acosta, *Assistant Editor*; Neri Garcia, *Interior Layout Designer*; Stephanie Reid, *Photo Editor*; Rachelle Cracchiolo, M.A.Ed., *Publisher*

Image Credits

Cover carsthets/Shutterstock; p.1 carsthets/Shutterstock; p.4 Monkey Business Images/Shutterstock; p.5 David R. Frazier Photolibrary, Inc./Alamy; p.6 Fivespots/Shutterstock; p.7 Tim Bradley; p.8 Lucian Coman/Dreamstime; p.9 Eric Isselée/Shutterstock; p.10 (top) Steve Byland/Shutterstock, (middle) Stephanie Reid/Vladimir Wrangel/Shutterstock, (bottom) Stephanie Reid/Radlovsk Yaroslav/Shutterstock; p.11 Daniel Hebert/Shutterstock; p.12 (left) Stephanie Reid/Andresr/ Eric Isselée/Shutterstock, (right) Eric Isselée/Shutterstock; p.13 Stephanie Reid/ Nanka Kucherenko Olena/Shutterstock; p.14 (top) Pickbest/BigStockPhoto, (middle) WENN/Newscom, (bottom) Stargazer/Shutterstock; p.15 (left) Stephanie Reid/Monkey Business Images/Shutterstock, (right) Worlds Wildlife Wonders; p.16 R. Brad Malone/BigStockPhoto; p.17 (top) Helen E. Grose/ Shutterstock, (bottom) Melissa Bouyounan/Shutterstock; p.18 Larsek/Shutterstock; p.19 (top) Photobar/Shutterstock, (middle) Markbeckwith/Dreamstime, (bottom) Olly/Shutterstock; p.20 (left) AFPlive/newscom, (right) Craig Dingle/Shutterstock; p.21 Two Blue Dogs/Shutterstock; p.22 Christian Musat/Shutterstock; p.23 (top) Javarman/Shutterstock, (bottom) Robert Photo/ Shutterstock; p.24 Stephanie Reid/Christopher Dodge/Rey Kamensky/Shutterstock; p.25 John Lindsay-Smith/Shutterstock; p.26 Art Explosion; p.27 (top-left) Jurgen Kleykamp/Dreamstime, (top-right) Emin Kuliyev/Shutterstock, (bottom-left) Ke Wang/Shutterstock, (bottom-right) Jordi Espel/Shutterstock; p.29 David R. Frazier Photolibrary, Inc./Alamy

Teacher Created Materials

5301 Oceanus Drive
Huntington Beach, CA 92649-1030
http://www.tcmpub.com
ISBN 978-1-4333-0427-9
© 2011 Teacher Created Materials, Inc.
Reprinted 2013

Table of Contents

A Day at the Zoo

Today our family is going on a trip together.

We are going to the zoo. We want to find out what animals are long, tall, short, and small.

Looking at Animals

The python moves by stretching out. It bunches up its middle. Then it pushes its head forward.

LET'S EXPLORE MATH

Look at this snake. How many cubes long is it?

An adult python gets to be quite long. If Dad could lie down next to it, they would be about the same **length!**

Hippos stay in shallow water all day. They are too heavy to swim. Once it cools off, they eat for about 6 hours.

The food a hippo eats in a zoo would fill one wheelbarrow. It eats hay pellets and grass. Hippos like fruit for dessert.

Look at those teeth! They never
stop growing. They can even grow
as long as my arm!

I looked hard to find this tiny bird. Some hummingbirds **weigh** less than a dime!

LET'S EXPLORE MATH

Hummingbirds drink a lot of nectar. They need to eat five times their weight. This hummingbird weighs the same as a nickel.

Look at this hummingbird and the quarter. Which weighs more?

Hummingbirds are very fast. They are the only birds that can fly backwards. They can also **hover**. They can even fly upside down.

Gorillas are about as tall as Dad. But they weigh a lot more than Dad weighs. A male gorilla weighs about the same as 3 men.

A gorilla may eat 40 pounds in 1 day. That is about the weight of my five-year-old sister.

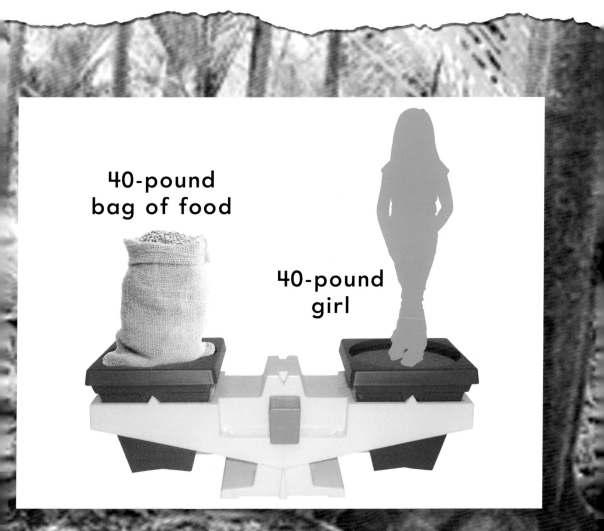

40-pound bag of food

40-pound girl

A newborn panda is the size of a stick of butter. The adults are much bigger. They may weigh more than a large person.

Pandas eat **bamboo** 12 hours a day. That would be like waking up at 7:00 and eating almost until bedtime!

Pandas eat up to 80 pounds. That is more than you weigh!

Polar bears have a thick layer of fat. It helps keep them warm in the cold water.

They love to eat seals in the wild. At the zoo, polar bears eat dog **kibble** and fish. Peanut butter is their favorite treat.

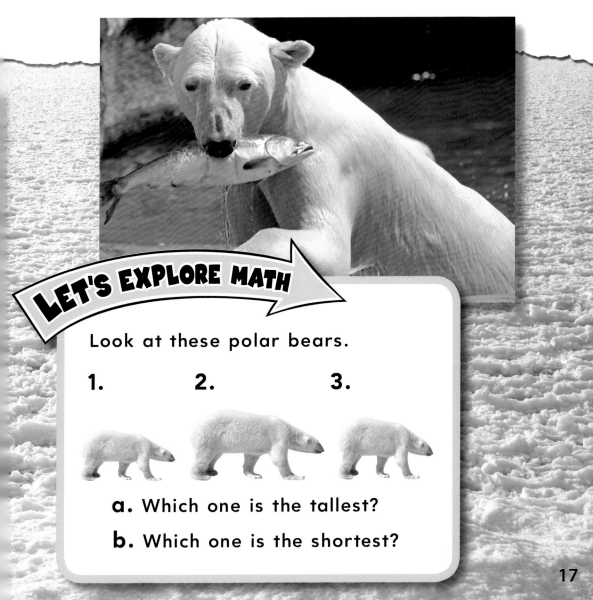

LET'S EXPLORE MATH

Look at these polar bears.

1.   2.   3.

a. Which one is the tallest?

b. Which one is the shortest?

Mom tells us to think of being in a fast car on the highway. That is how fast a cheetah can run.

A cheetah's spine can bend. It can stretch its front legs out very far. That long **stride** lets it **sprint** after prey.

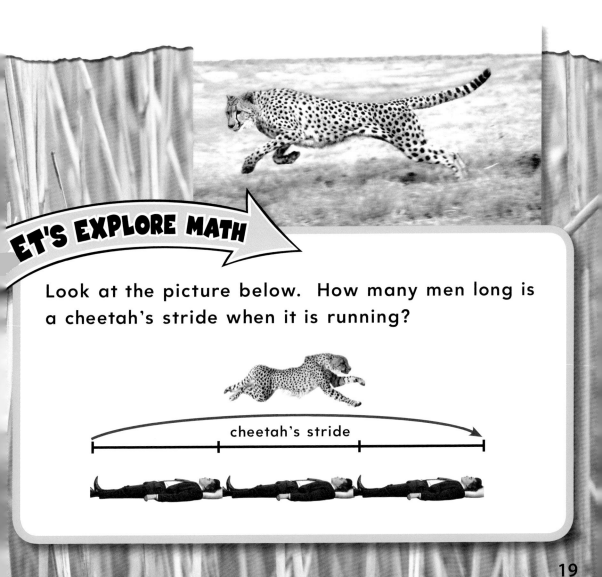

ET'S EXPLORE MATH

Look at the picture below. How many men long is a cheetah's stride when it is running?

cheetah's stride

A baby kangaroo is called a joey. It may be smaller than a honeybee when it is born. An adult is the same size as Dad.

Its feet are as long as my arm. Its tail is even longer. It can hop higher than Dad's head.

The tallest animal at the zoo is the giraffe. It could look into a second floor window. Its legs are as tall as Dad. So is its neck!

Giraffes eat leaves all day with their long tongues. They also eat carrots and hay at the zoo.

LET'S EXPLORE MATH

A giraffe has a long tongue. Look at the picture. Some of the tongue is inside the mouth. How many cubes long is a giraffe's tongue?

Elephants are huge! A male can weigh about the same as 3 pickup trucks. They eat hundreds of pounds of leaves and **bark** in the wild each day.

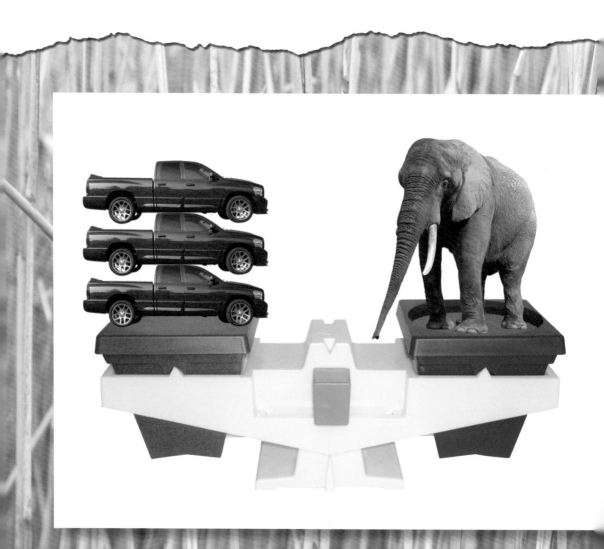

At the zoo they eat hay, leaves, and fruit. They flap their big ears to keep cool.

A Great Day

We finish our day by thinking about the animals we saw. Some were tall and some were short. Some were heavy and some were light. But they were all fun to see!

LET'S EXPLORE MATH

bear   giraffe   hippopotamus

hummingbird

Look at the animals above. Put the animals in order from shortest to tallest.

We want to do what all animals like to do after a long day. Take a long nap!

Feeding Animals

Jack helps out at the zoo during the summer. He has to choose the containers that are used to feed the animals. He looks at the chart for help.

What the Animals Eat

Animal	Food	Container
pythons	small mice	
hummingbirds	sugar and water mix	
polar bears	fish	
kangaroos	plant pellets	
elephants	leaves	

This is his list of containers.

- 1 garbage can
- 1 bucket
- 1 bottle
- 1 small pan
- 1 large bowl

What container should be used to feed each animal? Copy the chart. Choose which container could hold each type of food.

Solve It!

Use the steps below to help you solve the problem.

Step 1: Think about what each animal eats.

Step 2: Think about what can go into each container. For example, which container would best hold fish?

Step 3: Think about the size of the animals. If they are big animals, they need big containers.

Step 4: Choose a container for each animal. Then fill in the chart.

Glossary

bamboo—a tall, treelike grass

bark—the outside covering of the branches and trunk of a tree

hover—to fly in the air without changing direction

kibble—a dry form of pet food shaped into pellets

length—the measured distance from one end of an object to another

sprint—to run at top speed

stride—the distance covered by a step

weigh—to measure how heavy or light an object is

Index

Let's Explore Math

Page 6:
27 cubes

Page 10:
the quarter

Page 17:
a. 2
b. 1

Page 19:
3 men long

Page 23:
25 cubes

Page 26:
hummingbird, hippopotamus, bear, giraffe

Solve the Problem

What the Animals Eat

Animal	Food	Container
pythons	small mice	small pan
hummingbirds	sugar and water mix	bottle
polar bears	fish	bucket
kangaroos	plant pellets	large bowl
elephants	leaves	garbage can